MW00441986

THE MAGIC OF HERBS

THROUGHOUT the AGES

With a special section
devoted to Old Time,
Household Herb Formu-
lae, Herb Teas, Strange
and Curios Herbs, Roots
etc.

By Henri Gamache

All rights to this book have been purchased from Marvel BookCo.

Published in 1985 by:

ORIGINAL PUBLICATIONS
22 East Mall
Plainview, New York 11803

BIBLIOGRAPHY

The author is indebted to the following Authors, Works, Herbals and Manuals for the legends, traditions, customs and practices which have been associated with Herbs since earliest civilization. Recipes, Formulas, Classification of Herbs according to their therapeutic values, etc. have been set down verbatim.

Flower Lore and Legend, Mrs. Katherine Beals
Plant Lord, Legends, Lyrics, Richard Folkard
Myths and Legends of Flowers, Charles Montgomery Skinner
Herb Magic, Occult Review (vol. 37), H. Stanley Redgrove
De Hortorum Cultura, R. Rapin
Folklore of the Northern Countries, W. Henderson
The Herbal, or General Historie of Plantes,
        F. Gerarde (Edited by Samuel Johnson 1633)
Natural History, Pliny
The British Physician, Robert Turner
Encyclopaedia of Gardening, F. C. Louden
La Mythologie des Plantes, A. De Gubernatis
The British Herbal, N. Culpeper
De Mirabilibus Mundi, Albertus Magnus
De Luce et Umbra, Ars. Magnetica, Kicherus
Popular Names of British Plants, Dr. Prior
The Herbalist, Joseph E. Meyer
Secretum Secretorum, Aristotle
Official National Formulary
The Golden Bough, Frazier
De la Demonomaine de Sorciers, De Jean Bodi (1580)
The Herbal, W. Turner
Autobiography, Cellini

PART I

HERBS IN HISTORY

Chapter I

The Ancient Medicine Man or Witch Doctor

The whole history of modern medicine is founded upon herbs, plants, trees and flowers. Nature, in her infinite wisdom, has provided a whole storehouse of natural remedies to cure the ills of all mankind. It has simply remained for man to discover them and to put them to good use.

The therapeutic value of botanicals as compared to man-made chemicals is open to argument but one big argument in their favor is that the former are *natural* agents and harmless in the ordinary dose which is more than can be said of many chemicals.

In our Grandmother's day common, everyday remedies were always "home-made". Tonics, cough syrups, laxatives, liniments were all made in the kitchen "laboratory". Rhubarb and soda, syrup of figs, for a laxative; honey, cherry and white pine cough compound, elderberry and blackberry wine; Snake

Root, Mayapple and Indian Turnip Liniment — are but few of those home-made remedies that we still remember.

The reader will perhaps wonder who first discovered the medicinal value of herbs, roots, plants and flowers. The answer to that question is hidden in antiquity — lost in the dawn of history. Perhaps, however, the following explanation comes as close to its solution as any.

Away back, when civilization was young, the first inhabitants of the earth were vegetarians, feeding on grasses, roots, berries and herbs. Those that agreed with them they continued to eat while they stayed away from those that made them ill.

Later when man learned how to make a fire and to eat the roasted flesh of animals, he lost much of his knowledge of herbs and roots and plants. Meat, to him, was the important thing in keeping his hunger appeased. So he began to domesticate animals, sheep, goats, cattle.

Those early shepherds of the hills still remained close to mother nature, however, and had many opportunities of studying nature all around them. They had plenty of time to experiment with various plants and soon learned by observation the results from eating these various plants.

Gradually these aboriginal men became the Medicine Men of their tribes. Because of their superior knowledge of various roots, they were able to prescribe brews and concoctions to cure the ills of brother tribesmen. Each time a cure was effected, the value of the medicine man was increased to his tribe — and accordingly so was his power.

The ancient medicine man jealously guarded his secret knowledge and passed it on to his eldest male offspring who, through generation after generation added more and more knowledge and experience to his art.

Witch Doctor or Medicine Man of the Malekula Tribes of the New Herbrides Islands in the South Seas

Gradually, other members of the tribe were wont to believe, that in some way, the powers of the Medicine Man were bound up with the Gods and Goddesses which they worshipped

This belief that there was some religious significance to the power of the Medicine Man was increased by the fact that he often chanted over his brews, or made incantations or made signs or performed rituals. This he did to make the patient believe that it was his personal power that brought about the cure — NOT the natural herbs which he concocted. At the same time this was the one means he had of keeping secret his formula for the cure.

Thus it came about that the early tribesmen thought that some magic power rested with the Medicine Man and soon his advice was sought on all matter of subjects — some of them far removed from the curing of bodily ills.

If a tribesman sought to overcome a personal enemy, he went to the Medicine Man who perhaps prescribed an herb which made the offender violently ill. Sometimes he even gave potions of poison brew to entirely eliminate the undesirable one.

Of course, payment was always exacted for such services until the Medicine Man became among the wealthiest in the tribe.

Thus a form of Witchcraft and Sorcery was established which, after many generations, became a part of the religion of these aboriginal tribes.

It is not to be wondered at that the Medicine Man or Witch Doctor was greatly feared and that great respect, which almost approached veneration, was tendered to him.

Even today, many of the cures effected by Medicine Men in Darkest Africa remain unexplained by modern science. The "Black Magic" of these Witch Doctors has been witnessed and described by competent observers yet they are without a scientific explanation.

Artist's conception of African Witch Doctor of about 1856

Chapter II

Herb Magic of the Early Israelites

As man grew wiser he gradually gave up his nomadic ways and began to settle down to live in one place. From the temporary camp, he came to live in villages and towns and soon began to be civilized. He built permanent homes; built ships for travel and trade and learned to write and to read; developed his morals and his religion.

Despite all this progress, man in the early days of civilization, continued to cling to many of the ancient ways. The Witch Doctor and the Medicine Man of the early days had disappeared but in his place were priests of the early religions. In their way they were as powerful as the earlier Witch Doctors had been.

There were many such priests who preyed upon the fancies of their people. Some, drunk with their powers were hated and feared. Others, more benevolent, performed great works for their flocks and were beloved and honored and became great leaders.

Such a man was Moses who, the earliest records of civilization reveal, exerted great influence over the early Israelites. The Bible records many instances of his great knowledge of Natural History and describes many of his formulae and recipes. His position as the religious head of his people enabled him to enforce his doctrines, his ethics, his rituals which he pronounced the "Law of God".

That they were natural laws, laws of common sense perhaps did not occur to his followers at that time.

Let it suffice to say that Moses was a wise man, more concerned with his people than with personal power. He had recorded all the laws and doctrines which he set forth and among them are found the earliest herbal recipes of mankind.

Some of these recipes of earliest civilization *still are in use today.*

Artist's conception of Moses receiving the 10 Commandments

Chapter III

Herb Magic of the Greeks and Romans

In all countries and in all climes there have been people who have depended upon the power of herbs, plants, trees and flowers. Many ancient races had their own particular sacred tree or plant.

For example the oak tree was the sacred tree of the ancient Celts and the Druids placed great store in the power of mistletoe which grows upon the oak. Even to this day the inhabitants of Wales call it *Prenawr*, "the celestial tree".

The Ash tree was sacred to the Norsemen; the Hindus and Brahmins had their "Tree of Paradise"; the Buddhists had their "Tree of Knowledge".

In the same way the ancient Greeks and Romans venerated both the oak tree and the ash. It was the belief of these ancients that man sprang from a tree. The Teutonic tribes of northern Europe had a similar belief.

The beliefs of these ancients had their origin in much the same way as those peoples in Africa and in the Orient. In many instances they came as stories or legends brought home by a Greek or a Roman who had traveled to some distant land. Often these stories were changed or modified to meet the conditions of the new users. Oftentimes the very plants or flowers or trees were transplanted to their new home for cultivation.

This is true of the Rose whose original home is said to have been Persia where it was held a sacred blossom of Love.

Some ancient Greek or Roman seeing this beautiful flower, and remarking upon its fragrance and learning of its alleged power as a talisman of Love, perhaps brought it back to Greece and Rome where it was cultivated and grew in importance as a Symbol of Love.

The Greeks were the first of the early Europeans to develop the arts, literature, philosophy and even science to a fairly high degree. The pages of history are filled with the names of Greeks who were wise beyond their time. Socrates, Plato, Aristophanes, Aristotle are but a few of these early wise men.

The Romans, on the other hand, were very much unlike the Greeks. Whereas the Greeks were great thinkers and philosophers and artists, the Romans were warriors and law givers.

What religion, and philosophy and medicine they had was largely stolen or copied from the Greeks. Thus it is not strange that the Herb Magic of the Romans should be so like the Herb Magic of the Greeks.

Among the great Greek Philosophers, perhaps there was no greater name than Aristotle who was born in 384 B.C. and died in 322 B.C.

When he died at the age of 63, he left hundreds of philosophical writings which have profoundly affected civilization even to this day. He thought about and wrote on all manner of subject: Religion, Ethics, Morals, Biology, Natural History, Botany, Astronomy, Physics, etc., etc.

Among his more famous works was his *"Natural History"* and his *"Secretum Secretorium"* in which he sets forth many ideas, many explanations, many discoveries and many formulae.

He set down his *"Golden Cabinet of Secrets"* which composed, in part many formulae, recipes and customs. He, like many other philosophers of his day, kept many things secret because he feared that some of the information and many of the customs — if they become too widely accepted — would be misused to the consequent disadvantage of the nation.

Among these formulae and recipes were certain herbs and

plants which he and his fellow philosophers had studied and found to be poisonous or narcotic in their influence. Aristotle knew that this information in unscrupulous hands could cause wholesale murder or degradation of many of his people — so he withheld this general information and gave it only to a few of the more responsible of his students.

In his pursuit of the study of medicine and anatomy Aristotle made many discoveries about herbs, plants and flowers.

An Ancient Manuscript

He found that some were *Astringents*, which had a tendency to contract tissues. Others he found were *Antispasmodics*, which helped prevent the recurrence of spasms and relieved muscular irritability. He found some Demulcents, which soothed irritated mucous membranes of the nose and throat and thus were good for coughs and colds, etc.

In addition to tonics, sedatives, aromatics, laxatives and purgatives he also wrote about many which were stimulating in their action. Because of the limited knowledge and experience available Aristotle was not able to tell WHY certain herbs brought about certain results. He could only tell WHAT results could be expected.

When he observed, for example, that a given herb would act upon the glandular system of an aged patient in such a way as to make him or her feel more youthful, he immediately set it down as a Love Powder or Love Philtre.

At that period in Greek history there were no Universities as we know them today. Rich men sent their sons to a tutor or a philosopher, who lectured to a few students and taught them all he, himself knew. After a period of such tutoring — which extended over a period of from four or eight years or even longer, .the student himself went forth to pass on the knowledge he had learned together with some of his own ideas, discoveries and philosophies.

It is not to be wondered at therefore that many of the discoveries, the ideas, philosophies, formulae and recipes of the Great Aristotle should have come down and be used all through these many years — even to our own day.

The fame of the great philosopher spread all over the world. His original secret recipes were used in Rome, in

Alexandria, in Cairo. Many of the famous people of history used them in their original or modified form.

Cleopatra was said to have used a "fatal fragrance" which made men powerless to combat her wiles. It is thought that this was nothing more than a fragrant incense which, when burned in the right setting was conducive to peace and quiet or to romance.

History has recorded that her chambers were filled with beautiful odors, where rare incenses burned all the time and that it was her custom to anoint her body with fragrant oils so that those who might enter her chambers would believe that they were near a beautiful flower. If these are the facts, it is no wonder that Mark Anthony was drawn to her exotic chambers to become enslaved by her physical charms.

The fatal fascination which Cleopatra held over men was as old and mysterious as the Sphynx

An incense such as Cleopatra might have used is the formula which follows:—

Winter's Bark	16 ounces
Sandalwood	24 ounces
Orris Root	8 ounces
Patchouly Leaves	8 ounces
Myrrh	8 ounces
Olibanum Tears	8 ounres
Wood Base	8 ounces
Saltpeter	2 ounces
Light Pink Coloring	2 ounces

The above herbs, leaves, bark and resins are ground together into a powder and burned. Some people like to take a small piece of charcoal and light it and sprinkle the powder thereon.

The odor of this incense is exotic in its fragrance. One book to which we have had access lists this as "Cleopatra's Incense"

Today we know that incense is soothing and quieting to some peoples' nerves. We know, too, that each perfume has a personality all its own and may be alluring, seductive, exotic. sensuous, carefree, etc. Used intelligently it can "create a mood or an atmosphere".

Despite the great advances which civilization made during the time of Aristotle, education and knowledge was for the rich and favored few. The great masses of people still remained ignorant and to a great extent superstitious.

The greater the works of the really informed, the greater the magic in the eyes of the ignorant. When they were given an herb for the treatment of some condition, they were kept uninformed as to what it was. When it accomplished its purpose it was still the result of the doctor's "Magic" as far as the patient was concerned.

This was a period, then, during which civilization made its first great strides and during which many famous philosophers and early scientists sprang up. They added much to the world's knowledge by their discoveries, their formulae but the average man still lived in a world which venerated the Magic of Herbs.

Chapter IV

Legends and Traditions of Herb Magic
in Winning and Holding Love

We have seen in previous chapters how all through the ages "Magic" was used for curing all sorts of bodily ills. The "Magic" was nothing more than ignorance of the actual facts. The well informed used herbs and roots and plants to accomplish a specific purpose but the uneducated masses actually thought that some magic rites were being performed to cure them of their malady.

Gradually, it was reasoned, if the Witch Doctor could perform miracles to cure bodily ills, why not cure ills of the spirit and of the heart? Why could the Witch Doctor not foretell or inspire the affections between the sexes? Why not be able to bring back a wandering lover; why not arouse passion within the breast of one who was loved?

Perhaps in no period of history did this phase of Herb Magic become so dominant as in the Middle Ages. Until at least the sixteenth century a curious form of sympathetic magic was generally believed in and practiced. If we are to believe the records of the times, and they certainly are voluminous, many "successes" were achieved.

Often when love turned to hate, when a suitor or husband or wife was forsaken a Witch was employed "to cast a spell" over the chosen one. Sometimes it was desired to prevent the consummation of a marriage with a rival; sometimes it was an attempt to compel the love and admiration of a particular person.

In each case whoever the subject and whatever the nature of the "spell" to be cast — whether fo. evil or good, there were other witches to cast spells to counter-act the alleged spell under which one was supposed to be laboring.

Badin writes that when he was Procurer-General at Poitiers, he had occasion to visit an alleged Witch who told him that she knew of fifty ways of Tying the Love Knot by means of "L'envoutement d'amour" which, translated literally, means "Magical Love Charm". In other words this particular woman perhaps had a considerable knowledge of herbs and their reaction on the human body. Because of this knowledge plus a possible knowledge of fortune telling etc., she gradually came to be known as a Witch who was adept in solving the love problems of those who came to her.

Badin, Cardan, Frazier all refer to "l'envoutement d'amour" and "denouement des noeuds" the untying of the marriage knot; When an Arab wife runs away, the pursuing husband ties knots in the grass to prevent her from "doubling back".

Artist's conception of a Witch "tying the knot"
as described by Badin

Love philtres and aphrodisiacs were used to such an extent during this period that at one time laws were passed imposing heavy penalties on those who used them to the disadvantage of the intended victim.

There were two kinds of concoctions which were most generally used, according to Hilda W. Leyel: "The love philtre was a concoction of herbs which, through its magical attributes or combined with them induced a feeling of love towards a particular person; whereas an aphrodisiac or "poculum amatorium" was composed of ingredients which conduced to a state of amorousness".

In one of his plays Rowlands gives a recipe for making turtledove powder which was said to stir the heart of her who drinks it. We quote the following:

"Take me a turtledove
And in an oven let her lie and bake
So dry that you may powder of her make
Which, being put into a cup of wine,
The wench that drink'st it will to love incline".

According to many Greek writers including Pliny and Aristotle, the aphrodisiacs of the Greek and Roman courtesans were made of pepper, myrrh and equal quantities of two scents called Cyprus and Egyptian, and that the cups from which these potions were drunk were made of scented earthenware.

Another Greek writer, Athenaecus, recorded that an Indian Prince presented Salencus with aphrodisacs which were of such strength that they immediately increased one's ardour when applied to the soles of the feet.

As has been mentioned in previous chapters, Aristotle's "Golden Cabinet of Secrets" describes in detail hundreds of formulae and recipes among which is one for making

THE TRUE LOVE POWDER

"Take elecampane (the seeds or flowers) vervain and the berries of mistletoe. Beat them, after being well dried in an oven, into a powder, and give it to the party you design upon in a glass of wine and it will work wonderful effect to your advantage".

Many other recipes for philtres, love powders and potions are found in ancient writings of Aristotle, Democritus, Paracelus, Albertus, Magnus, and others. Several references may be found in Shakespeare, for example when he attributes Othello's power over Desdemona to

> "Conjecture and mighty magic
>
> Thou has practis'd on her with
> foul charms,
>
> Abus'd her delicate youth with
> drugs or minerals
>
> That weaken motion".

*The use of Herbal love Potions
is as old as the Pyramids*

Among the English of Queen Elizabeth's day the roots of the sea holly or eryngo had earned a reputation for being a love tonic. A confection was made by coating the roots with sugar. These were sold under the common name of "Kissing Comfits". As late as the 17th Century these sweets were made and sold at Colchester, England by an Apothecary named Burton.

During the Renaissance — when sensual pleasures reached their peak in Venice, Rome and, in short, every part of Europe — Witches, Oracles, Apothecaries and others did a thriving business in love charms, "goblets d'amour", etc. Books were published and sold which contained all manner of recipes, some of them curious, some of doubtful value, many of them actually harmful.

Arhist's Conception of an Alchemist
of the Renaissance period.

Hilda Leyel is authority for the story that when Madame de Pompadour thought that she was losing the love of Louis the XV, she resorted to a tincture of cantharides. However, an overdose almost proved fatal. Only the fact that the Duchesse de Brancas found the bottle and recognized the odor saved her. Thereafter, it is said, Madame de Pompadour indulged in "chocolat a triple vanille" and celery soup—a far less harmful diet which she had prescribed for herself to correct her naturally cold temperament.

Alcohol sweetened with sugar is a common French restorative, according to H. W. Leyel, and it is said to have first been used to increase the ardour of the aged King Louis XIV. This is not wholly a French custom, however, for in several other countries it is still the custom to give a bride and groom cakes moistened with alcohol and sugar.

Literature abounds in references to Love Powders, Potions, Draughts and Brews and many famous personages in history other than those mentioned were said to have used them at one time or another. Among them are Josephine of Napoleonic fame, Cellini, Catherine the Great, Byron, Shelly, and many others. In some instances these people may have resorted to the use of habit-forming narcotics but hid their weaknesses under the guise of having had a Love Potion.

For example in Dryden's translation of Juvenal's "Satires", there is a reference to dissipators:

"Who lewdly dancing at a midnight ball

For hot eryngoes and fat oysters call".

Years later Byron makes mention of this passage and, according, to Leyel, the poet was said to eat hot eryngoes for their supposed tonic properties.

Napoleon believed that the nutmeg had great tonic and stimulating qualities according to several authorities and, both he and Josephine are said to have enjoyed a punch of hot milk, brandy and nutmeg.

Percy Bysshe Shelley, one of the greatest of English poets, was the wayward son of an English squire. At 19 he married a schoolgirl of 16. Later he married the famous Harriet Godwin. From his youth he lived life to the fullest so it is not to be wondered at that in 1818 at the age of only twenty-six he had to leave England to regain his health. He went to Italy and it is recorded that his quest for happiness did not outdo his quest for an "elixir of eternal youth".

He used many herbal concoctions with which he had become acquainted in England as well as many of Italian origin and he is said to have had constant recourse to a brew, the base of which was muskroot. Although Leyel credits musk with certain tonic properties, today it is credited with a soothing influence over the nervous system.

The Court of Catherine the Great was perhaps as licentious as any in the history of Europe and many were the practices indulged in by members of the courts.

Many Gypsy recipes were used — some of which perhaps had their origin in the Orient.

Among the Russians of that period the root of a certain fern was thought to have occult powers. Botanically the plant is called "aspidium flix mas" but in our time it has been called "Lucky hands" by some people because its unexpanded fronds resemble hands. Russians burned both the fronds and the roots and saved the ash, according to Leyel to "keep off spells of warlocks and witches". They related that Genghis Khan carried the ash in the secret compartment of a ring.

Catherine the Great was said to have drunk a brew made from the spa of this flowering fern in the belief that it would confer eternal youth upon her.

Benvenuto Cellini (1500-1570) was an incorrigible roisterer who went through life fighting, brawling, and philandering.

In his "Autobiography" he records many instances of

imbibing stimulants and various herbal potions. He records
that at one time hé was given poison in a sauce by Sbietta,
Duchess of Florence which deprived him of his vigor for a
full twelve months. During this time he resorted to stimulating restoratives, among which was a cordial distilled from
the fermented roots of the crocus.

Those who sought herbal philtres whether for their own
use or for dispensing to others usually believed that Magic
made them successful even though such herbs as were employed in them were considered of an erotic nature and were
often combined with cantharides medicinally. Among the
herbs thus used were vervain, jasmine, coriander, cyclamen,
purslane, maiden hair, valerian, navelwort, wild poppy, anemone, crocus, periwinkle, pansy, carrot, lettuce, endive and
many others. In Part II of this volume will be found addi-
tional details concerning each of these specific herbs.

Certainly it was a common belief of that time that the
more Magical or Occult Herbs that a person utilized the better their chances for success.

Perhaps the only limit set upon the use of many herbs was
their great cost. Some herbs of that long gone era were more
valued than jewels, and it would have taken almost a king's
ransom to purchase every kind of herb available for the alleged purpose of securing amatory favors.

Nevertheless, there were many who used mixtures of
herbs — as many as their purse would permit — which were
carried on the person. At first these were carried in a small

bag around the neck. Later in a jeweled receptacle such as a locket which usually took the form of a heart, which since earliest times has been an Amulet of Love.

Ancient Greeks and Romans were particularly partial to the myrtle and a water made from the flowers and leaves has been used in practically every country. A well known American Herbal published as late as 1934 states that the roots of the myrtle should be collected late in the fall, cleansed thoroughly and while fresh the bark separated with a hammer or club. The bark is then dried and kept in a dry place. Thereafter it is pulverized and the resulting powder kept in a dark sealed vessel. Myrtle has both astringent properties and stimulating properties. The astringent qualities are extracted by boiling in water while the stimulating properties are extracted with alcohol.

The famous Angel Water of the eighteenth century which originated in Portugal used extract of Myrtle as a base. H. W. Leyel is authority for the following recipe which her long research on the subject led her to:

ANGEL WATER

"Shake together a pint of orange flower water, a pint of rose water and half a pint of myrtle water. Add 2/3 of distilled spirit of musk and 2/3 of ambergris. Heat spoils it and cold imprisons its perfume".

Leyel goes on to say: "Mandragora (mandrake), henbane, dragon's blood and satyrion, particularly the last, were all cited with lustful properties. The mandrake is mentioned in the Old Testament as a cure for sterility and the belief is endorsed by the Doctrine of Signatures. Circe made use of the mandrake in her love potions while in Persia the herb is recommended to secure a husband's love".

The Chinese, for the same reason and for the same purpose, use ginseng root. Sir Edwin Arnold, in describing the ginseng says: "It will renovate and re-invigorate falling bodily powers beyond all other stimulants, stomachicks and energisers of vitality. The Korean people believe the sard root to be absolute panecea for all mortal ills mental and physical. From sixty to ninety grains of the dried root are a proper dose; it fills the heart with hilarity whilst its occasional use adds a decade of years to the ordinary span of human life".

The Chinese, too, knew the value of herbs

There is a legend among the Persians that a certain recipe could be used for regaining the affections of a loved one. This was composed of cloves, cinnamon and cardamoms. According to the directions given these were placed in a jar and over it was read seven times backwards the "Yasin" chapter of the Koran. The jar was then filled up with rose water. The husband's shirt was then steeped in the brew. This procedure was said to insure the return of a husband. Of course such a fantastic ritual could have no basis in fact but it is merely set forth as typical of some of the absurd beliefs of pople in some distant lands.

In the preceding paragraphs we have given numerous illustrations and legends which tend to show how the herbs were used to stimulate love or affection but there were those who sought herbs which had a tendency to quench or subdue love.

Dr. Short in his famous "Herbal" says that the monks, nuns, friars and hermits of a bygone period who would live chastely, used herbs like the water-lily, the poppy and the hemlock which were said to deprive the taker of all desires.

Both Galen and Anicenna recommended a poultice of hemlock to abate the ardour of love while the German Alchemist, Adrian Mynsicht set down a formula in the seventeenth century which he called "Water of Chastity".

PART II

Legends of Herb Magic

of

Fifty Important Plants-

In part I of this volume we have endeavored to give a brief, general historical outline of the use of herbs from the earliest days of man upon the earth. We have seen how a few informed people — whether Medicine Man, Witch, Alchemist, Apothecary, Monk or Philosopher — kept the masses in ignorance of the true value of herbs, plants, flowers and trees. Usually they were impelled by selfish motives; sometimes for really benevolent but strictly religious reasons.

Whatever the circumstances, this condition has prevailed year after year, century after century down to our own day when many patent medicines with herbal bases are made and sold.

Until the passage of certain laws within the past couple of years one did not know what he was buying beyond the maker's advertised claim. Today, however, new Federal Laws make it imperative to state upon the label the ingredients from which the medicine is made.

Truly this IS an age of enlightenment for now, if armed with a knowledge of herbs anyone may determine for himself whether he should risk the use of any prepared remedy.

Contrast this new found knowledge with the superstitions, the traditions of the past which were handed down by word of mouth from one generation to another. In the following pages we present for your edification many of these strange, exotic customs and beliefs — some based upon true facts, some pure fancy, a veritable Salmagundi which only the experienced researcher can separate into its component parts and say "true" or "false".

Although the reader who is desirous of making a collection of the herbs, roots and flowers hereinafter described may secure many of them from his local Supply House, it is always a wise precaution to assure oneself of the genuine article by purchasing a branded product such as the well known Amuluk Brand Products. This brand of Herbs is of uniformly high quality, sold in sealed packages and enjoys a wide distribution by established dealers.

If you are unable to secure a reliable brand of herbs just write the publishers of this volume, POWER THOUGHTS PUBLISHING COMPANY, Inc., 24 East 21st St., New York, N.Y. and you will be given the names and addresses of reputable Supply Houses who can fill your requirements.

ASTER

In the early days of England, the Aster was called "Starwort". R. Rapin in his "De Hortorum Cultura" mentions that the leaves of the Aster plant were used to decorate the altars of the ancient Celtic gods. He also says that the Starwort was a flower that was used by lovers as an oracle to determine whether their love is returned or not. He says that lovers were wont to use a formula and that in consulting the flower the following words were repeated:

> *"Er liebt nich von Herzen*
> *Mit Schmergen*
> *"Ja-oder Nein"*

As each leaf was pulled from the flower, the words "Ja" and "Nein" were repeated. The answer depended upon what word was pronounced when the last leaf was plucked. Those who have seen Goethe's great tragedy, "Faust" will recall that this same theme is found therein. Astrologists claim that the Aster is an herb of Venus who was the Goddess of Love. It is not to be wondered at therefore that the Aster has been considerd a Talisman of Love for many generations.

THE ASH

In previous chapters we have seen that in Norse tradition, it was thought that man sprang from the Ash tree. Perhaps this was due to the fact that the Ash is so imposing in the barren wastes of the Northland, the tree became symbolic of strength and vigor. There are legends to the effect that the first bow with which Cupid shot his arrow was made of Ash. With this symbolism, therefore, it is not to be wondered at that the Ash tree is closely connected with the love impulse. Folkard says in his book that in Cornwall, England, the leaf of the Ash tree is a talisman of good luck and in Henderson's "Northern Folk Lore" the following lines regarding the virtues of Ash leaves are found.

"The even ash leaf in my left hand.

The first man I meet shall be my husband

The even ash leaf in my glove

The first I meet shall be my love.
The even ash leaf for my breast.
The first man I meet's whom I love best
The even ash leaf in my hand
The first I meet shall be my man".
"Even ash, even ash, I pluck thee,
This night my true love for to see;
Neither in his rick or in his rear,
But in the clothes he does every day wear".

The Ash tree also was a symbol of generation, of love, in both Greece and Rome and Pliny often mentions it in such connections in his "Natural History".

BASIL

The Basil has a long and varied history and many legends have been told about it. To it have been attributed many potent properties as a Talismanic Charm.

Among the Hindus, Basil was one of the most sacred herbs with which they were acquainted. It is usually planted in the garden or court yard of the Hindu home where is it worshipped by all the members of the family. The pious Hindu invokes the divine herb to bring protection to every part of the body but above all to insure children to those who desire to have them.

*A Hindu Temple of Northern
India near the borders of Tibet*

According to Folkard, the Basil is regarded as an enchanted flower in Modavia. It is thought that the flower can cause a spell upon a wayward wandering youth and make him love the maiden from whose hand he grasps a sprig. A similar belief exists among Italians and Sicilians in our own time. The youths of Sicily wear a sprig of Basil behind their ear to denote the fact that they are of marriagable age and romantically inclined.

Gerard in his famous "Herbal" says that the odor of the Basil "removes melancholy and makes men glad and happy."

THE CARROT

In the reign of James I of England, it was a common practice for ladies of the era to adorn their headdress with leaves of carrots for the light feathery verdure was considered as a substitute for plumage. The ancient Greeks called it "Phileon" because of its connection with amatory affairs. In Gerard's "Herbal" which was edited by Dr. Samuel Johnson in 1683, it is remarked: "the carrot serveth for love matters; and Orpheus as Pliny writeth said that the use of the herb winneth love."

According to Galen the root of the carrot possesses the power of exciting the passions and it was thought if one dreamed of it, it signified profit and strength.

CORIANDER

From a passage in the "Book of Numbers" it seems that

this is one of the five herbs ordained by God to be eaten by the Israelites at the feast of the Passover. The Coriander was also highly esteemed by Hindus, Arabs and Egyptians. Its little round fruit is pleasantly aromatic and its seeds when they are covered with sugar are known as the famous Coriander Comfits. Robert Turner in the "British Physician" says that the powder of the seeds taken in wine seem to stimulate the passions.

CUMIN

According to Folkard this plant seems to have been regarded as especially possessing the power of retention. It was thought that whomsoever ate Cumin would be held steadfast in his devotion. In Italy it was placed in the pigeon's coop in order to aid in domesticating them at home. Country lasses in England also endeavor to make their lovers swallow it in order to insure their continued attachment and fidelity. It was thought that if a lover was going to serve as a soldier or attend work in a distant part of the country, and the sweetheart gives him a cup of wine in which Cumin has previously been powdered or mixed, he would remain faithful to his love.

CINNAMON

The spice known as cinnamon is the inner bark of the

tree, "Laurus cinnamonum", the leaves of which were used woven into wreaths to decorate the Ancient Roman Temples.

An oil which was extracted from the wood was used to annoint the sacred vessels used in religious rites. So highly esteemed was the bark especially in Arabia that only the priests were allowed to gather it.

According to Folkard the ancients used the flowers of the cinnamon tree to make a distilled water "which excelled in sweetness all the waters whatsoever" — presumably as an ingredient in love potions.

BALM OF GILEAD

The mountains of Gilead in the east of the Holy Land were covered with fragrant shrubs among them the "amyris" which yielded the celebrated Balm of Gilead. So potent was this thought to be that if a person coated his finger with it, he could pass it through fire without harm.

Because of this association, it was assumed that it could temper the fires of love or mend a broken heart. According to Skinner, throughout the East it is used as a skin beautifier and in the bath.

SANDALWOOD

In India, there grows a small tree which is celebrated because of its beauty and the perfume of its wood which is used in incense in the temples. The Chinese, the Buddhists, the Brahmins, the Burmans and Mussulmans all used Sandalwood with veneration. In the Burman Empire on the last day of their year which is April 12th, the ladies sprinkled Sandalwood mixed with rose water on all whom they met. This symbolized the washing away of the impurities of the old year and the starting of the new year without sin.

CYCLAMEN

The Greeks and the Romans had a number of different names for Cyclamen but regardless as to the name it was called, it was always regarded as a love plant. During the Middle Ages it was regarded as a potent assistant by midwives and it was recommended to them by the surgeons of the day. According to Theophrastus, Cyclamen was employed by the ancients to incite love and voluptuous desires. Potted and placed in one's bedroom, it was supposed to protect anyone who slept therein.

"St. John's wort and Fresh .Cyclamen

she in his chamber kept,

From the power of evil angels to

guard him while he slept".

DILL

Dill is an aromatic plant (antheum graveoleus). It is supposed by many authorities that its name was derived from the old Norse word "Dilla" which means dull. According to Folkard, Dill was greatly appreciated as a plant which had a tendancy to counteract any spells caused by witches and sorcerers. There were many who boiled it in wine which when drunk was reputed to excite the passions.

ENDIVE

According to the most ancient Greek Alexandrian translations of the Bible, Endive was another of the herbs which the Almighty commanded the Israelites to eat with lamb at the Feast of Passover. Even today, the leaves of this plant are used extensively in salads, while the roots of the plant are ground and mixed with coffee under the name of chicory. There are a host of love stories and legends which surround this notable herb, some of them have their setting in Germany, Switzerland, Poland, Greece, etc.

Folkard says, "All sorts of qualities have been ascribed to the Endive. It was thought that it should not be uprooted with the hand but with a bit of gold or a stag's horn. The Endive seed was used as a love philtre and it was taught that a girl uprooting an Endive as described above, would be assured the constancy of her love". Endive carried on the person is supposed by many to enable a lover to inspire the object of his affections with the belief that he possesses all the good qualities which she can possibly wish for.

ERYNGO

The seed Eryngo is perhaps better known as "sea holly". According to R. Rapin in his "De Hortorum Cultura", Eryngo possesses magical qualities inasmuch as if it were worn by a young married woman it insured the fidelity of her husband. Sappho, it is said, employed it in this very manner to secure the love of Phaon, the handsome boatman of Mitylene for whom Sappho had conceived so burning a passion that at length, mortified by his coldness, she threw herself into the sea. I quote the following lines from Rapin:

"Grecian Eryngoes now commence their
    fame,

Which, worn by brides, will fix their
    husband's flame,

And check the conquests of a rival dame.

Thus Sappho charmed her Phaon, and
    did prove

(If there be truth in verse) her
    faith in love"

FRANKINCENSE

A beautiful legend tells of the supposed origin of Frankincense. Leucothea who was a daughter of a Persian king was wooed and won by the God, Apollo. The king in order to avenge his stained honor ordered his daughter buried alive. Although Apollo was unable to save his lover's life, he sprinkled nectar and ambrosia over her grave which seeped through her body changing it into a beautiful tree which exudes a sap which becomes transformed into resinous tears. These are sold commercially as Olibanum tears.

The Egyptians as well as many other Orientals have made great use of it as a principal ingredient in religious perfumes and incense. Even to this day, it is used in some of the largest cathedrals in the world in religious ceremonies.

JASMINE

Jasmine is called by the Hindus "the moonlight of the grove". De Tassy has translated many of the allegories of Aziz Eddin in which the following appears: "Then the Jasmine uttered this sentence, 'that my penetrating odor excels the perfume of other flowers so lovers select me as a suitable offering to their mistresses'".

F. C. Louden in his "Encyclopedia of Gardening"

Old wood cut showing Jotham,
King of Judah, burning incense in the Temple ------ a
rite usually performed only
by the Priests of the   time
about 27 centuries ago

relates that in 1689 the Grand Duke of Tuscany procured the first double Jasmine blossom. He was so jealous of his blossoms that he forbade even his gardener to make a single cutting of them, but he was without calculcating that his gardener was in love. So, on the occasion of his sweetheart's birthday, the gardener gave his betrothed a sprig of Jasmine. Charmed by its fragrance the girl planted it and soon she had a whole gardenful of her own. Thus, she was able to sell blossoms at a high price. Before long, she had saved enough money to enable her to marry the poor gardener. To perpetuate this episode, the maids of Tuscany still wear a wreath of Jasmine on their wedding day and the custom has given rise to the saying: "the girl worthy of wearing the Jasmine wreath is rich enough to make her husband happy".

Folkard also quotes the common legend that if one were to dream of this beautiful flower it would certainly foretell of good luck while to lovers such a dream promised a speedy marriage.

BALM

The Melissa or Garden Balm was famous among Arabian Physicians who recommended it for " affections of the heart". According to Paracelus it promised a complete rejuvenation of man. Because of this it was often steeped in wine, and made an ingredient of love potions and brews.

ORANGE

There are certain writers who claim that the "golden apples" of Hesperides were really oranges. It is also believed that when the crafty Heppomenes beat Atalanta by causing her to stop and pick up the "golden apples" which he threw over his shoulder, he used oranges.

Greek mythology has it that Jupiter gave Juno an orange when he married her — thus it has become a bridal flower in many countries.

VIOLET

In Greek mythology there is a story that Jupiter was almost caught in one of his flirtations with Io, a priestess in Juno's Temple. Unable to conceal Io, Jupiter changed her into a white heifer; but since he considered that grass was not good enough for such a creature he also created the violet as her especial food.

In some manner, the violet became sacred to Venus and its perfume was said to be not only soothing but stimulating to the ardor of affection.

MULLEIN

The Mullein was, according to Folkard, formerly used by Wizards and Witches in their incantations. The plant was known as the Flannel flower from the fact that the stem and leaves are covered with a downy wool. Perhaps because of its association with Sorcerers of the day it came to be considered a love herb.

SWEET MAJORAM

This is one of those rare plants that gives spice and savor to meats. But inasmuch as it was thought to have certain antiseptic qualities it was largely used by the ancients for such reasons.

In Greece and Rome it was one of the hymenal flowers because it was one of the flowers which was dedicated to Venus the Goddess of Love. It was also said that it has the touch of the fingers of Venus that causes its perfume to linger . On the Island of Cypress they ascribe its origin to Amarakos who was a page boy in the household of a king. One day while carrying a jar of perfume through the halls he dropped the vase on the marble floor where it shattered to a thousand pieces. So terrified was the boy at the thought of the possibility of the king's anger that the very life went out of him and he lay there on the marble floor quite still bathed in the floral essence.

From his burial place there rose a beautiful plant which we know today as Sweet Majoram. This plant is also found in England and Germany and according to Skinner in his "Myths and Legends of Flowers" it was prized as a charm against witch-craft.

Sweet Majoram was considered to be a hymenal flower

HEMP

There have been many associations between Hemp and the British Empire. Folkard says: "In some parts of the country, in Cornwall on Midsummer's Eve and in Derbyshire on St. Valentine's Eve as the clock strikes 12, young maids desirous of knowing their future husbands go into a church yard and run around the church scattering Hemp seed and repeating the while without stopping these lines:

> *"I sow Hemp-seed: Hemp-seed*
>
> *I sow:*
>
> *He that loves me the best*
>
> *Come after me and mow".*

This sowing of Hemp seed is done by maidens at midnight on Midsummer's Eve in Cornwall, St. Martin's Night at Norfolk and at All Hollow's Eve in Scotland. The Sicilians, too, are said to employ Hemp as a "Charm to secure the affection of those whom they love".

A. De Gubernatis in his book, "La Mythologie des Plantes" tells us that on Friday, which is the day consecrated to our Lord's passion, the Sicilians take the Hempen thread and 25 needlefulls of colored silk and at midnight they braid this saying:

> *"Christu e cannara di Christu,*
>
> *Servi pi attaccari a Christu".*

Thereafter they go to church entering at the moment of consecration. Three knots are then tied in the braid to which has previously been added a little of the hair of the loved one. After this, they invoke all the spirits of the person to be loved to the person who craves his or her love.

THE HOUSE LEEK

The Old Dutch name for this was "Donderbloem" or "Thunderflower" because it was a common belief in the Middle Ages that the flower protected against thunder and lightning. Charlemagne at one time ordered it planted on every roof top. In Italy on Mid-summer's eve, rustic maids gather buds to represent their various lovers. Each one is tagged with a name of one for whom they have some affection. On the following morning that bud which has flowered the most during the night is said to indicate the future husband of the maid.

THE ROSE

At all times, in all countries, the Rose has been symbolic of Love and Devotion. In another part of this book, the origin and its subsequent cultivation all over the world is described, so we shall not go into the subject at this point. It is of interest to know that in Cornwall and Devon which are in England, it is believed that if a maid walks backward into a Rose Garden and plucks a rose and the rose is sewn into a paper bag and placed in a drawer until the following

Christmas, the maid may determine who will evenutally become to her husband. On Christmas morn the maid should remove the rose from its hidden resting place and place it in her bosom. It is thought that some young man will either ask her for the rose or take it from her on Christmas morn and that he will be her future husband.

VERVAIN

Vervain or Verbena has from time immemorial been the symbol of enchantment. Folkard says that the ancient Magicians employed this mystic herb in their pretended divinations asserting that by its use every wish could be granted. Vervain was one of the plants which was dedicated to Venus, the Goddess of Love.

In many rural districts of England, Germany, Italy — and in our own country, Vervain is still regarded as a plant possessing magical virtues as a love philtre.

It has, according to Folkard, the reputation of securing affection from those who take it to those who administer it. In Germany it was the custom to present a hat of Vervain to the newly married bride as though to place her under the protection of the Goddess Venus.

This plant was regarded by both Greeks and Romans as having the marvelous power of reconciling the bitterest enemies.

In many places it was the custom to steep the plant in water which then was used for cleansing houses in the belief that it would keep away evil spirits. This brew was known as "JUNO'S TEARS".

Beals also says that a few leaves were worn on the person as a protection from harm and states that the plant was venerated in Persia while magicians of the East used it is a symbol of enchantment. "They (the Persians) were responsible for the belief that if one smeared the body all over with the juice of the herb he would obtain anything that he might desire and be able to reconcile those who were at enmity"

It was the custom on Christmas Eve to build bonfires around which young men and women danced, wearing garlands of vervain. Any young woman who gave her lover a garland of Vervain thus insured his fidelity for at least a year. Even now the superstition of its efficacy as a love philtre has not entirely died out in England while Dr. Samuel Johnson wrote that Satan had no power over a maiden who wore vervain and St. Johnswort about her person.

Strangely enough students of the occult, the mystic and allied sciences are agreed that the Vervain ointments, and lotions of the ancient Greeks and Romans, the Verbena oils and washes of the mid-Victorian English and the Van Van oil of our Southern Negro all have a common hereitage. It is not to be wondered at therefore that Van Van Oil, Lotion, Wash, etc., find ready acceptance today — with almost 3000 years of traditions behind them.

ANEMONE

This flower is one of the earliest Spring blossoms. It is so fragile that it withers almost as soon as it is gathered. Anemone means "the wind flower" because some writers say that it is so fragile that even a wind blowing over it will cause it to wither. Others say that it only blooms when the wind blows it open.

There is a beautiful old legend based upon both of these thoughts which is worth repeating.

The story relates that Anemone was the name of a beautiful nymph whom Zephyr loved very dearly. Queen Flora became very jealous, however, and exiled Anemone from the Court where she pined away and died of a broken heart. Zephyr then importuned Venus who changed her body into the flower which bears her name and Zephyr is said to fan her all day long with his wings.

Pliny, in his "Natural History", attributes some medicinal properties to the plant while Beal in her book, "Flower Lore and Legend", relates: "Eastern magicians regarded the plant as a preventative of sickness and recommended everyone to gather the first blossoms that are seen in the Spring, repeating very solemnly the words: 'I gather thee as a remedy against disease'. Afterwards it must be wrapped in a red cloth and carefully kept in a dark place".

MUSTARD

In India the mustard seed smybolizes generation. According to custom a husband first tastes the seed and then his wife: "immediately, she who had been childless, conceives and nine months later gives to the world a daughter beautiful as a fairy".

MYRRH

Myrrh is a resin which is exuded by the Myrrh tree but it was held by the Ancients to have been the tears of Myrrha.

Myrrh is one of the ingredients of the sacred ointment or oil of the Jews with which the Tabernacle was annointed. It was used in the consecration of Aaron and his sons and was used in the purification of women as ordained by Jewish law.

Myrrh was always burned in the Temples of Iris who was the Egyptian Goddess of Love.

The white Narcissus is said to have originated with a mythical youth, Narcissus.

NARCISSUS

It had been foretold that this beautiful youth would be happy until he beheld his own face. Caressed and petted by the Nymphs and passionately loved by the unhappy Echo, he slighted and rejected all their advances. One day when heated by the chase, he stopped to quench his thirst in a stream. beholding his likeness in the water.

Becoming enamoured of his own beauty he became spellbound and pined away on the spot.

MANDRAKE

There are few plants which can boast such wealth of legend and tradition as the Mandrake. From the earliest times it was held in veneration by people of the East.

The leaves of the plant are dark green, hairy and pointed; the flowers a sickly white; the root shaped like a parsnip which is often forked, giving it an uncanny humanlike shape.

Medicinally, only the roots of the plant are used and they are gathered late in October or early November soon after the fruit has ripened.

The Greeks dedicated the plant to Circe, the golden haired enchantress who was the daughter of the Sun and celebrated for her witchcraft.

According to Beals, "In later times it was looked upon as a preventative of illness and all danger. Mountebank doctors carved the roots into idols, which were regarded as oracles and treasured as safeguards against evil. The power was also attributed to them of increasing money which was placed near them".

An Italian writer says that some of the ladies of Italy have been known to pay 25 to 30 ducats ($57.50 to $69.00) in gold for one of these charms.

The Mandrake

Reference to the Mandrake is found in the fourteenth verse of Chapter 30 of Genesis: "And Reuben went, in the days of the wheat harvest, and found mandrakes in the field and brought them to his mother Leah".

According to Pliny, the plant was credited with curative properties and it was commonly used for love potions.

The fruit of the Mandrake, when ripe, is like a Golden Globe and so it is sometimes called the LOVE APPLE.

In the United States it is found in many states and is known as the May Apple, Wild Lemon and Raccoon Berry.

Oddly enough our own American Indians were well acquainted with the virtues of the plant and modern physicians have recognized its value to the medical profession.

THE CROCUS

Legend says that this flower was named for a beautiful youth named Crocus who was consumed by his ardency of love for Smilax a sheperdess of the hills. Subsequently Crocus was changed into a flower which bears his name. The ancients often used to adorn the marriage bed with Crocus plants, perhaps because it was one of the flower, according to Homer, of which the couch of Jove and Juno was composed. The Romans at about the time of Nero were so fond of the Crocus that they used to strew their blossoms throughout their banquet halls and they also had them strewn in the fountains and small streams which flowed through their court yards, thus imparting a beautiful fragrance. Among the Romans, the Crocus was considered to be a great cordial and strengthener of the heart and it was said to excite ammatory desires.

NUTMEG

In the Middle Ages it was thought that Nutmeg, Cloves,

innamon and ginger all came from the same tree — a natural
result of Europeans having no first hand knowledge of this
oriental tree.

*The ancients believed that Nutmeg could
"overcome the Birds of Paradise"*

It was said that the strength of the Nutmeg in season was such as to "overcome the Birds of Paradise" so that they fell helplessly intoxicated. Because of this belief, Nutmeg was used as a stimulant in many potions, brews and especially in hot wine drinks.

MYRTLE

The Myrtle has more traditions woven about it than perhaps any other plant or herb which has come down to us today. One beautiful legend concerning the Myrtle is well worth repeating. There lived in ancient Greece, so the story goes, a beautiful maiden whose name was Myrene. A band of robbers murdered her mother, father and brothers and abducted her. Subsequently, she escaped and became one of the favored priestesses of the Goddess, Venus.

One day at a festival held in honor of the priestess, she discovered one of the murderers and Myrene's lover promised that if she would yield her hand to him, he would bring the robber band to justice. He was successful and he was rewarded by her; but Venus who became offended changed the bride into Myrtle which she ordained, as proof of her affection, should continue green and fragrant throughout the year.

The Myrtle therefore became an especial favorite of Venus and it was reputed by both the Greeks and Romans to have the virtue of preserving Youth and Love. April, among the Romans was a period of festivity and married couples always wore wreaths of Myrtle.

*In ancient times Brides
wore wreaths of Myrtle*

The plant was also associated with Hymen who was the son of Venus and it is therefore a symbol of unchaste love according to Folkard. History records the fact that Roman bridegrooms always wore Myrtle on their wedding day.

Many other manuscripts state that there was a tradition that to dream of Myrtle portended many lovers and a legacy. It was thought that if a married person dreamed of it, it indicated a second marriage and that generally speaking, it denoted a numerous family, wealth and old age.

THE YARROW

This plant has played an important part in incantations and charms particularly in the south and west of England, according to Folkard. Maidens are reputed to have resorted to the following method of love devination. The girl must first pluck some Yarrow from a young man's grave repeating the while the following:

> "Yarrow, sweet Yarrow, the first
> that I have found,
> In the name of Jesus Christ, I
> pluck it from the ground,
> As Jesus loved sweet Mary, and
> took her for his Dear,
> So in my dream this night, I hope
> my true love will appear".

Thereafter, she must sleep with the Yarrow under her pillow and it was said that her future husband would appear to her in her dreams. The Yarrow has also been called "nose-bleed" and we learn from Dr. Prior's "Popular Names

of British Plants" that it was used as a means of testing
a lover's fidelity. He quotes from "Forby" who in his "East
Anglia" says that in that part of England a girl will tickle
the inside of the nostril with the leaf of this plant crying:

> *"Yarroway, Yarroway, bear a*
> *white below;*
> *If my love love me, my nose*
> *will bleed now".*

Wad not go to clay".

The Yarrow is also known as "the old man's pepper"
and Scotch Highlanders as well as the Greeks made an
ointment and linimenet from it.

MUGWORT

The Latin name for this species of wormwood is "Ar-
temesia Mater of Heborum." It is thought that it was
named after one of the names of the Goddess Diana. Folkard says that it had the reputation among ancients as being
an efficient means of alleviating female disorders.

There is an old Scotch legend concerning a young maid-
en to the effect that:

> *"If they wad drink Nettles in March*
> *And at Muggins (mugwort) in May,*
> *Sae mony braw maidens*

Paul Barbette writing in the year 1675 says that if a girl slept upon a pillow under which a Mugwort rested, her whole future would be revealed to her..

CLOVES

The aromatic Clove tree is a native of Moluccas where it is very carefully cultivated by the Dutch. Its white flower is worn there as a mark of distinction. The Clove is considered one of the hottest and most acrid of aromatics. Gerard in his "Herbal" says that Portuguese women who live in the East Indies distill from the green cloves a certain liquor " of a fragrant smell which comforteth the heart and is of all cordials the most effectual".

POPPY

The origin of the Poppy was attributed by the ancient Greeks to the Goddess Ceres whose daughter Prosperpine had been carried away by Pluto. In order that she might obtain sleep and forget her great grief, she created the flower. Folkard says that Grecian youths and maidens endeavoring to prove the sincerity of their lovers, place a petal or flower leaf of the Poppy on the left hand. This was struck with the palm of the other hand. Upon contact, the petal broke with a sharp sound which denoted true attachment. If the leaf failed to snap, it signified unfaithfulness. From Greece this practice passed to Switzerland, Germany and other parts of Europe where it is still practiced.

ANGELICA

The very many benefits of this plant perhaps account for its name or perhaps, because of its sweet scented root, it was thought that it had the scent of angels and therefore obtained its name. Its old German name of "root of Holy Ghost" is still retained in many countries. The Laplanders believe that it tends to lengthen life and it is their custom to chew it like tobacco

CLOVER

While research reveals few authenticated myths about the Clover, it has been venerated and held in high esteem in many countries. The Greeks used Clover for decorations and garlands and the ancient Druids and the Celts held it in high esteem. Folkard says that a dream of a clover field meant Wealth and Prosperity while the Clover with *four* leaves instead of three has always been accepted as a token of Great Good Fortune. An old English verse suggests a formula to young maidens for ascertaining who their future husband will be. The verse goes:

"A Clover, a clover or two
Put in your right shoe,
The first young man you meet
In field, street or lane,
You'll have him or one of his name".

PANSY

This flower gets its name from the French word "pensees" which means "thoughts". The Pansy has been sung in song and story and many a poet has written of its loveliness.

Shakespeare, in his "A Midsummer Night's Dream", gives the pansy — which he called "Heart's Ease" — magical qualities. It will be recalled that Oberon bids Puck to procure for him "a little western flower" on which Cupid's dart has fallen and which maidens called "Love-in-idleness". The Pansy is said to be sacred to St. Valentine and is the special flower of Trinity Sunday. With such tradition surrounding the Pansy it is not difficult to see why it was considered a Talisman of Love.

PERIWINKLE

In France, the Periwinkle is considered emblematic of pleasurable memories and sincere friendship. It was said of Rousseau that one day upon seeing a Periwinkle plant he recalled all the memories of his friendship with Madam de Warens even though more than 30 years had elapsed in the meanwhile.

N. Culpeper in his "British Herbal" says that the Peri winkle is owned by Venus and that "the leaves eaten together by man and wife cause love between them".

ELECAMPANE

R. Rapin in his "De Hortorum Cultura" writes:

"Elecampane, the beauteous
Helen's flower,
Mingles among the rest her
silver store:
Helen whose charms could Royal
breasts inspire
With such fierce flame as set
the world on fire".

These famous lines were perhaps inspired by the tradition that when the beautiful Helen of Troy was carried off by Paris, it was said she carried in her hand a nosegay of the bright yellow flowers which was thereafter named "Helenium" in her honor.

The Elecampane is a flower of the Aster family and is sometimes called "Scabwort".

In modern medicine the root of the plant is used, from which tonics and gentle stimulants are made. Thus we see that modern science has proved the useage to which the ancients put the plant.

The Romans employed the root as an edible vegetable and Folkard states that the ancient monks, who knew it under the name of "Inula campana", considered it capable of "restoring health to the heart".

Turner in his "British Physician" calls it the Sun Flower and in addition to indicating several medical uses, says that distilled water of the green leaves makes the face fair.

PURSLANE

According to Folkard this is an occult plant which in olden times was considered a sure protection against Evil Spirits. It was said to have been strewn in and about the bed to insure happiness in the home.

MAIDEN HAIR FERN

Anyone who is familiar with this plant knows that if it is placed under water it takes on a silvery appearance and when removed it will be found to be perfectly dry. Water will not cling to it.

The ancients saw in this peculiar property a magic symbolism. They claimed that this plant was the hair of Venus, for had not the Goddess of Love risen from the sea? According to Roman symbolism the plant was conducive to producing Grace, Beauty and Love.

Artist's conception of Venus
rising   from   the   sea

MAGNVS · ALBERTVS · BOLSTADIVS · COGNOMENTO

Multa pedumq̃, oneri tibi quondam Alberte, fuerunt
Dulcius est Sophiæ delituisse sinu.

Old woodcut of the great
Albertus Magnus

VALERIAN

The old herbalists of the Middle Ages noted that cats were fond of the roots Valerian. It was said that they even dug up the roots and rolled upon them as they did in catnip. Anyone who has observed the effect of catnip upon a cat will have noted the seemingly mild and pleasant intoxication in the animal.

The Great Albertus Magnus in his "De Mirabilibus Mundi" states that Valerian yields "certain juices of amity, efficacious in restoring peace between combatants and inducing harmony between husband and wife".

SATYRION

The name of this plant is derived from the Greek "Saturos" or Satyr and is applied to several species of orchis, from their reputed aphrodisiac character.

The Romans believed that the roots of these plants formed the food of the satyrs. In Gerard's "Herbal" we read that most of these plants were used for the purpose of exciting the amatory passions.

Turner in his "Herbal" says that all the species of Satyrion have a double root which alter every year "when one waxeth full, the other perisheth and groweth lank". The full root, he says, powerfully excites the passions, but the lank ones have the opposite effect.

Kircherus in his "De Luce et Umbra, Ars, Magnetica, Etc."
states that Satyrion was a favorite herb with Magicians,
Witches, Sorceresses and Herbalists who held it to be one of
the most powerful incentives to amatory passions.

He relates the case of a youth who, "whenever he visited
a certain corner of his garden, became so inflamed with pas-
sionate longings; that with the hope of obtaining relief, he
mentioned the circumstance to a friend who found that the
place was over-grown with Satyrion; the odour from which
had the effect of producing amatory desires".

ROSEMARY

In Europe in the Middle Ages — and even at a later
date — it was customary for brides to wear the Rosemary on
their wedding day while the bridal bed was decked with its
blossoms. Mystically it was believed that the Rosemary
strengthened both memory and the heart and that it signified loyalty, devotion and love.

According to Beal a certain charm utilizing the Rosemary
was thought to be extremely potent.

On the Eve of St. Magdalene — so the tradition went, let
three maids gather in the bed chamber of one of them and
prepare between them a mixture of wine, vinegar and water
in a glass vessel. Each maid must take three sips of the liquid

into which she must dip a spray of Rosemary which is then placed in her bosom. Then all must go to sleep in the same bed without breaking silence for a single spoken word will suffice to break the charm.

It was said that the dream of each — if the conditions are kept would reveal her fate.

Gerard in his "Herbal" extolls the virtues of the Rosemary: "The flowers made up into plates with sugar after the manner of Sugar Poset and eaten", he writes, "it comforteth the heart, and maketh it merie, quickeneth the spirits and maketh them more lively".

The belief in the sovereign virtues of Rosemary is a very old one and it was one of the ingredients in Roger Bacon's celebrated "Recipe for the Cure of Old Age and the Preservation of Youth".

DRAGON'S BLOOD

Dragon's Blood is not a plant but rather a product of the Calamus draca, a species of palm tree found in Sumatra and Borneo. The fruit is the size of a large cherry and is covered with scales. When it ripens a red resin exudes from the fruit which is gathered and dried to make Dragon's Blood.

There are two commercial types of Dragon's Blood —the

reed or stick and the lump. The former is wrapped in palm leaf while still soft and is considered the finer of the two types. According to C. F. Leyel, Dragon's Blood is still used as a Love Charm and as an ingredient in cosmetic preparations.

Dragon's Blood
wrapped in palm leaf

PART III

Recipes and Formulae

In this section we present numerous recipes and formulae which we have gathered from many Herbs. Books on Cosmetic Chemistry, Manuals of Incense and Perfume and other similar works.

These are set down exactly as originally recorded. We make no claims for their authenticity nor do we make any statements concerning their alleged beneficial effects.

Many of these formulae and recipes will be recognized as old family remedies which were used with results by former generations.

SUCCESS INCENSE

Ancient writings record that among the early Israelites it was the custom to burn incense in order to obtain Success in their various ventures. According to Beal, an incense burned to obtain success came to be known as Success Incense. A formula which has been handed down for this purpose follows:

Powdered	Sandalwood	30%
"	Myrrh	10%
"	Patchouly Leaves	5%
"	Orris Root	5%
"	Cinnamon	10%
"	Frankincense	40%
"	Saltpeter	3%

ATTRACTION INCENSE-

Woodbase	32	ounces
Olibanum	16	"
Sandalwood	8	"
Myrrh	4	"
Cinnamon	8	"
Orris Root	4	"
Saltpeter	2	"

All of the above ingredients should be in powdered form. Blue color should be added.

BIBLE INCENSE

This is a type of incense which has been widely sold under the above name. The ingredients follow:

Powdered Olibanum	....	24	ounces
" Sandalwood	....	8	"
" Myrrh	....	8	"
" Charcoal	....	14	"
" Woodbase	....	32	"
" Saltpeter	....	2	"

COMMANDING INCENSE

Winters Bark	16	ounces
Sandalwood	16	"
Orris Root	8	"
Patchouly	8	"
Myrrh	8	"
Olibanum	8	"
Woodbase	16	"
Saltpeter	4	"
Purple Coloring Matter	2	"

VAN VAN INCENSE

Woodbase	32	ounces
Myrrh	4	"
Cinnamon	8	"
Olibanum	12	"
Sandalwood	12	"
Vervain	4	"
Yellow Coloring	2	"

VAN VAN ANOINTING OIL

1 ounce	Soluble Oil Base
2 drams	Vervain Essence
2 drops	Yellow Coloring

JOHN THE CONQUEROR OIL

1 pint	Soluble Oil Base
2 ounces	Jasmine Bouquet
6 drops	Yellow Coloring

1 John the Conqueror Root in each bottle

MAGNET OIL

1 ounce	Soluble Oil Base
2 drams	Orris Bouquet
2 drops	Brown Coloring

Place 1 Lodestone in each Bottle

ORIENTAL LOVER'S SACHET

10 ounces	Plain Talcum
1 ounce	Powdered Orris Root
1 ounce	Magnesium Carbonate
4 drams	Jasmine Bouquet

Deep Pink Coloring

CAMPHORATED OIL

Mineral Oil   100 grams

Camphor   10 grams

Heat under a low flame until camphor is dissolved.

SUN TAN OIL

Peanut Oil   5 ounces

Sesame   5 ounces

Mix thoroughly and add perfume to suit.

A SKIN TONIC

800 C. C.   Water

200 C. C.   Alcohol

10 C. C.   Borax Acid

5 C. C.   Glycerine

2 C. C.   Perfume to suit

Mix well and filter.

PRESSING OIL
which is often called
HAIR STRAIGHTENER

Oil—

Amber Petrolatum	100 grams
Light Mineral Oil	20 grams

Cream—

Amber Petrolatum	100 grams
Parafene Wax	120 grams

Melt together, add perfume to suit. Pour into jars and allow to cool.

Famous among Early American Indian remedies are the Old TAMARACK REMEDIES. These native home remedies have been used for several generations and still find favor among a great section of our people.

CANADA SNAKE ROOT LINIMENT

For muscular soreness, stiff neck and wherever a hot, penetrating liniment is useful:

1 ounce	Canada Snake Root (Wild Ginger)
1 "	Capsicum
1 "	May Apple Root (Mandrake)
1 "	Indian Turnip (Dragon Root)

Place the ingredients in a vessel containing two quarts of water; boil down to 1 quart and add a handful of soap shavings. When dissolved, strain and liniment is ready.

GREAT SPIRIT TEA

Meyer's "Herbal" (1940) says "This is truly a great remedy containing botanicals that could be found in the pocket of many an Indian Medicine Man as well as in the medicine chests of the early settlers. It was found useful in feverish conditions associated with head colds and seemed to induce perspiration by opening the pores".

2 ounces	Boneset Leaves
1 ounce	Juniper Berries
2 ounces	Elder Flowers
1 ounce	Wild Ginger
2 ounces	Sweet Flag Root

Place the above 2 quarts of water, boil down to one 1 quart Dosage; 1 cupful hot upon retiring.

PALEFACE BOTANIC TEA

This tea was used by the Indians and pioneers. It is a mild tea and said to be particularly useful in conditions where it is advisable to employ a stimulant diuretic to the kidneys to produce better elimination through the urine.

1 ounce	Sassafras
4 ounes	Horsetail Grass
2 ounces	Cheese Plant
1 ounce	Elecampane
1 ounce	Bull Nettle
1 ounce	Gravel Plant

Grind all above ingredients and place in vessel containing two quarts of water; boil down to 1 quart and drink at least a pint a day.

SPRING TEA

This is one of the old fashioned Spring Tonics. It has been handed down from generation to generation and has been considered a valuable formula. Its action is slightly laxative. Composed of equal parts of the following herbs:

Sassafras, brak of root

Red Clover Flowers

Turtlebloom Leaves

Tinn. Senna Leaves

Fennel Seed

Aise Seed

PART IV

HERBS, THEIR CLASSIFICATION AND USE

In giving the therapeutic value of the botanicals which follow, it should be understood that the properties indicated as well as their classification are not our own opinions but data taken from such sources as Herbals, and other books on Materia Medica.

It should be thoroughly understood that in every case of aliment it is advisable to consult your family physician. He may and often time does, prescribe botanicals to suit the particular case at hand.

Many patent medicines are made from Botanicals. It is an established practice to divide each formula into six parts:

3 parts Active Drugs

1 part Aromatic Drugs

1 part Demulcent

1 part Laxative

Following are listed many herbs, according to their medical properties. The list is not a complete one by any means because a volume of this character does not permit a complete list. The herbs mentioned are merely given to show the great number of botanicals which find use in our daily lives.

LAXATIVES

These are herbs which stimulate secretions of the intestinal glands or excite moderate peristalsis promoting mild evacuation.

Licorice Root	Tulip Tree
Cascara	Golden Seal
Black Butternut	Senna Pod
Turtlebloom	St. John's Bread
Snakehead	Dandelion Root
Yellow Poplar	Yellow Root
Blue Gentian	Rhubarb
Flax Seed	May Wort

PURGATIVES

These are herbs which have an action similar to LAXATIVES except that they are far stronger and induce copious evacuation.

Mandrake Rhizome	Senna Leaves
May Apple Root	Buckthorn Bark
Boneset Herb	Black Root

AROMATICS or CARMINATIVES

These are herbs which for the most part are pleasant and pungent to the taste and are useful to expel gas from the stomach and intestines. They are chiefly used to make other drugs more palatable and to prevent griping in catharitics.

Anise Root	Angelica Root
Cloves	Celery Seed
Canada Snake Root	Sassafras Bark
Wild Ginger	Elecampane Root
Coriander Seed	Peppermint
Yarrow Herb	Spearmint
Cardamon Seed	Caraway
Cumin Seed	Parsley Root
Catnip Herb	Sweet Clover

NERVINES

The following herbs seem to have a soothing influence on nerves that have been subjected to undue excitement or strain.

Fragrant Valerian	Celery Seed
Lady Slipper	Mistletoe
Blue Scull Cap	Rosemary
Blue Vervain	Mugwort
Catnip Herb	Kola Nuts
Hop Flowers	Sweet Basil
Musk Root	Wild Lettuce

TONICS

The following herbs seem to be popular with women as meeting their particular or peculiar tonic needs.

Pappose Root
(Blue Cohosh)
Palmetto Berries
Lovage
Bearberry
Alder
Squaw Vine
Squaw Root
Rosemary

Liferoot
Shepherd's Purse
Queen's Delight
Pale Cohosh
Beth Root
Elecampane Root
Angelica Root
Tansy
blue Cohosh

STOMACHICS — TONICS

These are herbs which promote nutrition and tend to tone up the stomach. Past generations have found them useful in loss of appetite and associated conditions.

Blue Gentian
Columbo
Wild Cherry Bark
Wild Sage
Wild Strawberry
Angelica Root
Congo Root
Chicory Root
(Endive)
Waywort
Solomon Seal
Chocolate Root

Dandelion Root
Elecampane
Ginseng Root
Golden Seal
Thyme
Juniper Berries
Blackberry Root
Wild Sarsaparilla
Jamaica Ginger
Mugwort Herb
Quassia

ANTHELMINTICS

These are herbs which are said to help expel worms from the stomach and intestines. Those in the first column seem to be best, it is said, for tape worms.

Malefern	Elm Bark
Pomegranate	Flax Seed
Pumpkin Seed	Wormwood

EXPECTORANTS

Expectorants are herbs which modify quality and quantity of mucous secretions and favor its expulsion. They are the chief ingredients of medicines for common colds and coughs as well as irritations of the throat.

Hoarhound	Nettle Leaves
Butterfly Weed	Solomon Seal
Balm of Gilead Buds	Wild Cherry Bark
Seneca Root	White Pine Bark
Life Everlasting	Wahoo Bark

DIURETICS

These are herbs which are used in medicines which promote the secretion of urine. Generally speaking they are used when the kidneys are not sufficiently active. Most people have a tendency to use Diuretics to excess thus over stimulating the kidneys.

Seven Barks	Sweet Bugle
Trailing Arbutus	Dog Grass
Watermelon Seed	Corn Silk
Burdock Seed	Beth Root
Dwarf Elder Bark	Juniper Berries
Indian Chickweed	Birch Leaves
Pipsissewa Leaf	Skunk Cabbage
Horse Radish Root	Parsley Root
Pimpernel	Kava Kava

ASTRINGENTS

These are herbs which tend to contract the tissues. The following are used in medicines for such a purpose.

Black Alder Bark	White Oak Bark
Blackberry Bark	Alum Root
Water-lily Root	Butternut Bark
Maidenhair Fern	Kola Nuts
Hawthorn Berries	Iron Wood
Life Everlasting	Billberry
Mountain Ash Bark	Gold Thread
Black Cherries	Sweet Fern Root
Black Willow	Swamp Snake Root

FRAGRANT BOTANICALS

The following herbs, roots and barks are used in Sachet

perfumes, Incense mixtures and in the manufacture of certain Flavors and Perfumes.

Lavender Flowers	Wild Ginger
Master of the Wood	Wintergreen
Tonka Beans	Deer Tongue
Cloves	Sandalwood
Cassia Bark	Rose Petals
Penny Royal	Orris Root
Gum Myrrh	Peppermint
Wild Vanilla	Tansy Herb

COLORING HERBS

The following herbs were widely used by the Indians but now are only occasionally used in toilet prepartions, hair tonics, etc. .The name of the herb is given as well as the color which it makes.

Madder	Red
Sage	Green
Saffron	Red
Walnut Hulls	Brown
Golden Seal	Yellowish
Red Saunders	Red
Sumach Leaves	Brown
Blue Malva	Blue
Alkanet	Red
Henna Leaves	Yellow
Black Malva	Black
Blood Root	Red

STRANGE and CURIOUS BOTANICALS
Sometimes Called AMULET HERBS

Although some of these herbs have medicinal properties, they are set down because they have been and still are used by many people who believe that "herbs bring good fortune". Sometimes the herbs are placed in a bag and carried around the neck. Sometimes one herb is used, often times a combination of herbs which seems to please the fancy of the particular individual.

The writer makes no supernatural claims, but merely lists some of the better known and more popular herbs of this classification.

Devil Shoe String	Dragon's Blood
Loveage Root	Sea Spirit
Five Finger Grass	Oriental Gum
Master of the Wood	Sacred Bark
Southern John the Conqueror	Adam and Eve Root
	Tonka Beans
High John the Conqueror	Queen's Root
	Orris Root
Queen Elizabeth Root	Cumin Seed
Grains of Paradise	Wahoo Bark
Life Everlasting	Alkanet Root
Holy Herb	Sumbul Root
Jezabel Root	Bethel Nut
Buckeye	Holy Sandalwood
Lesser Periwinkle	

Learn to Work with Natural Magic

_____ Draja Mickaharic_____

A Century of Spells

A collection of over one hundred useful spells . . . that work!

By the author of the best-selling Spiritual Cleansing

A CENTURY OF SPELLS by Draja Mickaharic

This book is a practical introduction to natural magic.It is a work book designed to help you learn magic, and it can serve as a practical reference for any practicing magician. You will work with many different kinds of spells from a number of different magical practices.This will give you an overview of the field of natural magic so you can decide if you want to work with the advantages and limitations of the magical art. You will learn protection spells, and also how to reverse spells that have been directed at you. The author provides complete instructions for working with water spells, baths, sprinkles, incense, oils, and herbs. He has included some spells of Obeah and Wanga, spoken spells, and a host of interestingspells-such as the Seven Knob Wishing Candle Spell, Four Thieves Vinegar, Lodestone Spells, how to work with bath salts, and how to make your own Obi stick. The instructions are clear, and the author shares his personal experience gained from working with these spells, so you know they are tried and true. By the author of the best selling "Spiritual Cleansing".

5 1/2"x8", 168 pages, paperback $7.95

THE WITCH'S FORMULARY AND SPELLBOOK
by Tarostar

A book of formulas and spells previously available only to a few people. A curious combination of Voodoo and witchcraft. This book describes the spells and the materials used in these spells. A valuable addition to anyone's collection.
Illustrated, 6"x9" 102 pages, paperback $6.95

THE MAGIC CANDLE by Charmaine Dey

The object of this book is to help you understand what you are doing, and to create and develop your own techniques and rituals which will surely bring you the results you desire. It doesnt matter what your religion is. You really don't have to be religious (or anti-religious) at all.
Illustrated, 5 1/2"x 8", 62 pages, paperback $3.95

READING YOUR FUTURE IN THE CARDS
by Louise Woods

Discover the extraordinary powers of an ordinary deck of playing cards. You'll be fascinated as you learn what each card means, the importance of positioning them, and how combinations reveal startling surprises. Go for the unknown. Astound your friends! Become a *Reader Extraordinaire!*
Illustrated, 4" x 6", 144 pages, paperback $3.95

HELPING YOURSELF WITH SELECTED PRAYERS

Compiled and translated from Spanish by Original Publications. Over 100 prayers that have helped people with all types of problems. Over 40,000 copies of this book are in print.
5 1/4"x8", 68 pages, paper $3.95

VOODOO & HOODOO by Jim Haskins
Their Traditional Crafts
Revealed by Actual Practitioners

VOODOO MEN, HOODOO WOMEN & ROOT DOCTORS,
say they know how to use eggs, graveyard dust; pins and
nails; red flannel bags; yellow homespun; urine, feces, and
blood;shoes and clothing; black cats and black hens; door-
steps; and the interior and exterior corners of houses to
conjure good and to conjure evil. Voodoo & Hoodoo tells how
these spiritual descendants of African medicine men and
sorcerers "lay tricks" and work their and explains the hold
these practices have had on magic, their believers, from the
Old World origins until today. Voodoo and its variant among
black Americans, Hoodoo, are still practiced. These are the
stories and secrets of the hoodooers, voodoo women, and
root doctors who serve paying customers all over the country right now in small southern towns and large northern
cities. Her are the "recipes" they use to attract a man or a
woman, to keep a over faithful, to avoid the law, and to win
at numbers. Here's how they use graveyard dust to cast
powerful spells, and the uses theymake of High John the
Conqueror root, Luck-in-a-Hurry Incense and many other
items, to work signs, uncross tricks and gain power over
others. A privileged survey of conjury in the American black
subculture, Voodoo & Hoodoo traces the phenomenon from
it's African roots to it's practice in Africa today.
51/2"x8", 226 pages, paperback $8.95

THE MASTER BOOK OF CANDLE BURNING
or How to burn candles for every purpose.
by Henri Gamache

"How can I burn candles in a manner which will bring me the most satisfaction and consolation?"

In order to answer that question it is necessary to sift and sort every fact, scrutinize every detail, search for the kernel.

It is to be hoped that this volume answers that question in a manner which is satisfactory to the reader. It has been necessary, of course, to include some historical data and other anthropological data in order to better illustrate the symbolism involved in modern candle burning as practiced by so many people today.

This data has been accumulated from many sources; it has been culled from literally hundreds of books and articles. The modern rituals outlined here are based upon practices which have been described by mediums, spiritual advisors, evangelists, religious interpreters and others who should be in a position to know.

It has been the author's desire to interpret and explain the basic symbolism involved in a few typical exercises so that the reader may recognize this symbolism and proceed to develop his own symbolism in accordance with the great beauty and highest ethics of the Art.

This book is a classic, many books have imitated it, but it is the original. *The Master Book of Candle Burning* has been in print for more than 50 years. It has been read and purchased by many thousands of people all over the world. *Original Publications* has had over 50 thousand printed in the last 5 years. It is a must in the library of every person interested in magic.

5 1/2"x8 1/2", 96 pages, $3.95

AWO
Ifá and the
Theology of
Orisha Divination
by Awo Fá'Lokun Fatunmbi

Throughout time people of diverse cultures have sought information to help them live their lives. Tarot, bone oracles, I Ching, playing cards, cola nut and tea leaves were among the sources consulted. The information obtained was used by the seeker to bring balance back into their world.

Within the Yoruba spiritual system the casting of sixteen cowries provides a finite tool that begins a transformation process that can lead to the healing of the seeker's concerns. Each throw of the shells brings forth an odu that begins to manifest immediately and continues as the diviner and seeker do the rituals the odu prescribes.

I have observed this process and its profound effect upon both diviner and seeker. For the diviner, there are always doors of knowledge being open through each reading that can lead to a deeper understanding of Orisha. The seekers learn how to develop spiritual balance as they work through their issues. Diviner and seeker can also experience their faith in action, bringing a deepening of their belief in Orisha.

Awo: Ifá and the Theology of Orisha Divination offers diviner and seeker a firm foundation in Yoruba divination. Also Awo reveals the Yoruba method of dilogun and gives initiated practitioners another way to use this oracle.

5¼"x8" 240 pages paper $12.95
ISBN 0-942272-24-2

Ìwa-pèlé
IFÁ QUEST
The Search for the Source
of *Santería* and *Lucumí*
Awo Fá'lokun Fatunmbi

"*Ìwa-pèlé* blends belief and skepticism, intellect and emotion to give us the beauty of African mysticism and the power of western thought. Only a few white men have made a true effort to understand and embrace African Spirituality, Herskovitz, Griaule and Bascom. Now let us add Awo Fa'lokun." **LUISAH TEISH** *Author of, Jambalaya: The Natural Woman's Book of Personal Charms and Practical Rituals*

Ìwa-pèlé is an excellent introduction to *Ifá* religion. The modern Yoruba accent in this book has gracefully demonstrated Fatunmbi's remarkable talent for expressing quintessential African religion, which I agree to.
The taste of the pudding is in the eating.
Ire o. (Cheers) **ADEBOLU FATUNMISE**

5¼x8 214 pages Paper $11.95
ISBN: 0-942272-23-4

SPIRITUAL CLEANSING by Draja Mickaharic
A Handbook On Psychic Protection

This book is a manual of psychic first aid, written to help you clean your spiritual atmosphere and to protect yourself in your environment. Everyone, at some time or another, has met an individual who seems to be surrounded with negativity, or has visited a place that seems imbued with "bad vibrations". Removing these negative vibrations is what spiritual cleansing is all about. With this book you will be able to solve most of the problems of day to day negativity that may be encountered with people, places and things. It teaches how to clean away the psychic drudge in your environment, how to clean the previous tenant's vibrations out of your house or apartment, how to remove vibrations from secondhand furniture or clothing, how to cleanse your own aura. The author's "household formulas" include recipes for herb, nut and flower baths for healing, reducing tension, increasing mental acuity, bringing love into your life, or even for economic improvement. He shows how to use incense and flowers to sweeten the home and clear the air after arguments. He discusses ways of using sea salt to help invalids or children, and the efficacy of eggs to ease physical pain and for protection while asleep. These simple and effective solutions to common psychic problems are presented in a way that allows the reader to take care of his environment without spending years studying magic.
5 1/2"x8", 97 pages, paperback $5.95